Requires Windows 95
or Mac 8.6 or higher

All About Me
Creative Clip Art for Classroom & Home

Created & Designed by Dianne J. Hook

ISBN 1-59441-191-3

Contents

Credits

Illustrator: Dianne J. Hook
Project Director: Jennifer Weaver-Spencer
Content Design: Sherrill B. Flora, Jennifer Weaver-Spencer
Cover Production: Annette Hollister-Papp

Clip Art Assembly Basics

Here are some suggestions as you make projects using clip art from this book.

Tools

Putting together the right tools will make your project go more smoothly and look better in the end. A good **copy machine** is a must. It's worth the extra effort to make sure your school or copy shop has machines that make clean copies. You will also need a bottle of white **paper correction fluid**, a fine-tip **black marker** to combine designs and add your own art to the project, **rubber cement** to mount the design onto your paper during the layout stage of your project, and **scissors** for cutting apart the designs you choose. Optional tools to help create a professional-looking project are a **nonreproducible blue pencil**, to make marks that will not show up on copies; a **proportion scale**, to help you determine the size of the reduction or enlargement necessary to fit your paper; and **blue grid paper** for laying out the project with straight lines.

Assembly Instructions for Creating a Page with a Lined Handwriting Template

1. Lined handwriting templates can be found on pages 4-6 of this book. Choose the template that is most appropriate for the writing abilities of your students. Then, select a decorative border page.

2. Make copies of the lined handwriting template and border of your choice. Cut the lined handwriting template to fit inside the border. Use blue grid paper or a light table to make sure that you have properly centered the writing lines. Attach the template to the inside of the border with doublestick tape or rubber cement.

3. Try to keep a ¼-inch margin on all edges of your paper. If the cutting edges from the lined handwriting template are visible on your first copy, lighten the copy machine setting by one notch. Alternatively, use correction fluid on the first copy, and then use that copy to make the final pages for your students.

Hints

- Keep a ¼-inch margin on all edges of your paper.
- If the edges of the cutout pieces are visible on your copies, lighten the copy machine one notch or use correction fluid on one copy and then use it to make the final copies.
- Removable tape is great for creating layouts if you will be using the design more than once.

Using Clip Art on CD

Journal pages presented in black and white in this book are available in color on the enclosed CD. If desired, the images can be easily layered to create other pages. The CD is Mac and PC compatible.

All About Me!

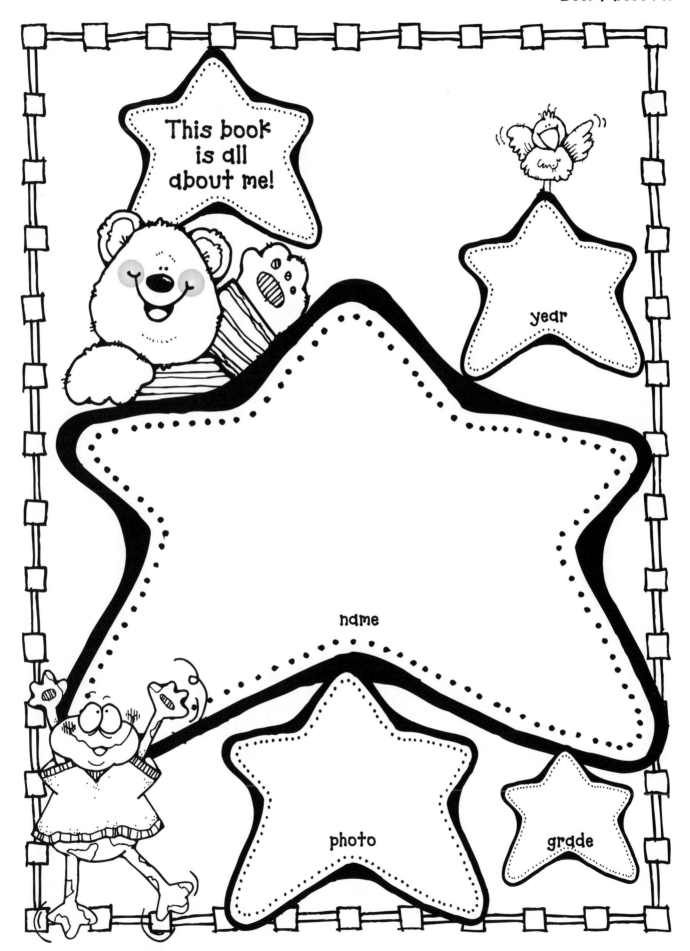

This book is all about me!

year

name

photo

grade

Some facts about ME!

I'm this tall _____

I weigh this much _____

I'm this age _____

9

My Paw Prints

Draw or stamp your handprints here.

_____

date

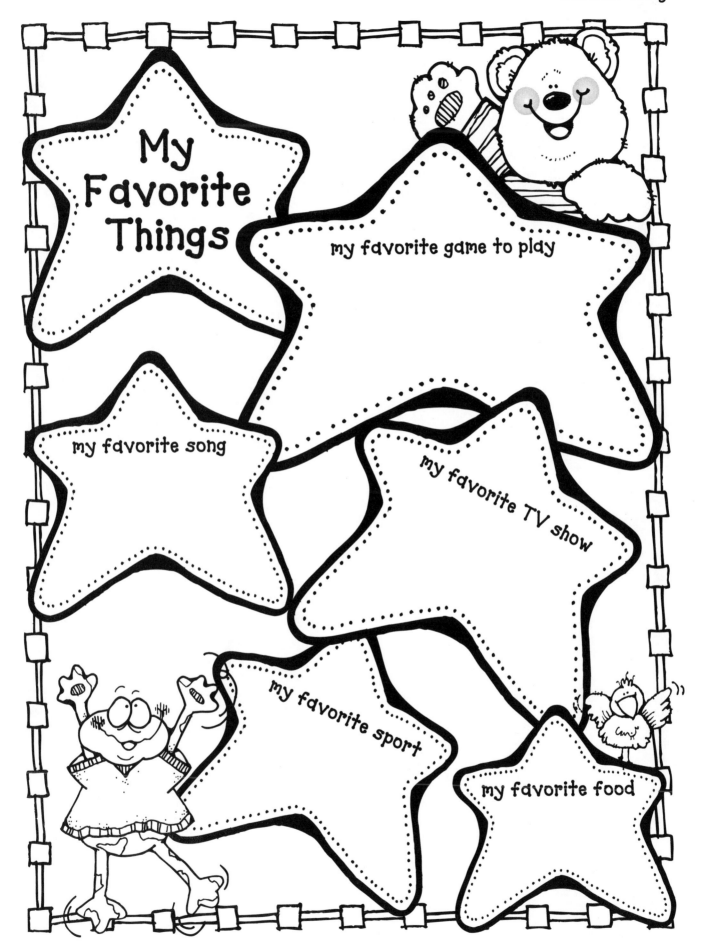

My Favorite Pet & Animal

My Teacher

School Subjects I Like

14

My Favorite Food

Some of my favorite games to play are

Creative Me!

Sometimes, I just AMAZE myself!

When I grow up, I want to be

Dare to dream!

The movie
I like best

Here's what I do for fun

My Birthday!

My Family

My family is

Birds of a feather flock together.

23

A little story about my family

Home Sweet Home

Draw a picture of
where YOU live.

I love to collect

My classroom at school looks like this

Draw a picture of your classroom
and YOU at your desk.

What I like to do during recess

Special Field Trips

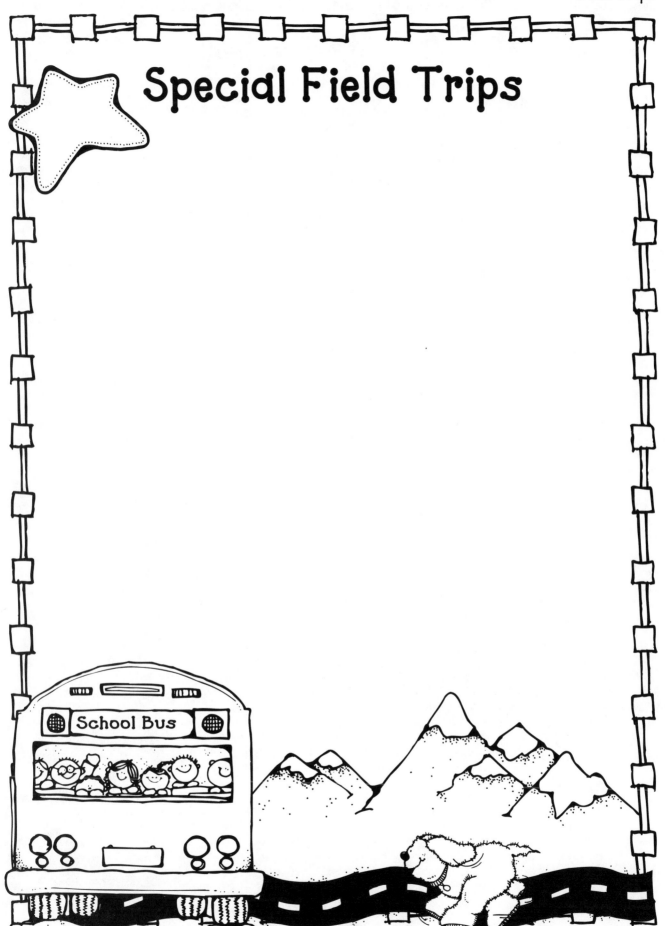

School Bus

Awards & Prizes

Lessons, Lessons, Lessons

List some of the lessons or classes
you take after school
and why you take them.

31

My Buddies

My Best Friend and Me!

I like to stay in touch with

This person really made a difference to me

Draw a picture of and tell a story about someone that has made your life better.

What I did on my summer vacation

The best vacation I've been on is

What makes me
SMILE

Just for Fun

Autographs

Teachers ✦ Friends ✦ Helpers

January Happenings

February

February Happenings

42

March Happenings

April Happenings

44

May Happenings

June Happenings

Strawberry

July Happenings

August Happenings

September Happenings

October Happenings

November Happenings

December Happenings

Use this clip art to help
YOU create other
fun scrapbook pages.

Bear Border

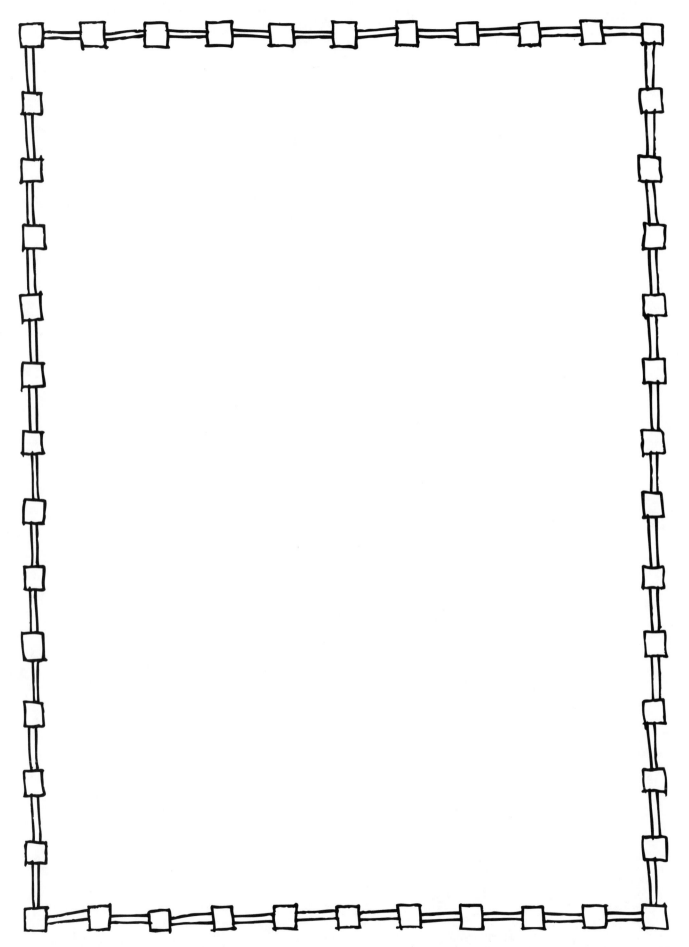

allaboutme_b

apple_b

applehalf_b

april_b

august_b

autographs_b

awards_b

awesome_b

awesomezig_b

backpack_b

balloon_b

balloonbunch_b

bannerbday_b

bannerfroggie_b

bannermedal_b

bdaybear_b

bearbrdr_b

bestfriend_b

bigpencil_b

bird_b

birthday_b

birthdaybold_b

bookboutme_b

books_b

border_b

camera_b

classroom_b

collections_b

creativeme_b

december_b

facts_b   familyis_b   famstory_b   favfood_b   favgames_b   favmovies_b

favthings_b   favpet_b   february_b   fieldtrip_b   forfun_b   froggie_b

frogstackbrdr_b   grownup_b   hibear_b   home_b   intouch_b   january_b

july_b   june_b   justforfun_b   ladybug_b   lessons_b   march_b

may_b   medal_b   mybuddies_b   myfamily_b   myteacher_b   november_b

october_b pawprints_b persontome_b present_b recess_b schoolbell_b schoolhouse_b

schoolhousewsun_b september_b smile_b star_b starfrogbrdr_b subjects_b

sumvacation_b sun_b vacationbest_b